CYBERSECURITY
TIPS FOR MID-SIZE
LAW FIRMS

An Easy-to-Understand Guide for
Managing Partners, IT Managers,
and Firm Administrators

Tom Lambotte

Cybersecurity Tips for Mid-Size Law Firms:
An Easy-to-Understand Guide for Managing Partners,
IT Managers, and Firm Administrators

Book cover and layout by Sadie Butterworth-Jones

CONTENTS

A LETTER FROM THE AUTHOR

Dear Readers,

As we enter the digital age, law firms face new challenges and risks that come with technology advancements. With sensitive data at risk, law firms must protect themselves from potential cyber threats while still managing their operations and serving their clients.

In my discussions with managing partners, firm administrators, and IT managers, I've confirmed the difficulties of implementing comprehensive cybersecurity strategies while running a law firm. However, with this book, I aim to simplify this process and provide you with easy-to-implement tips that will move your firm towards better cybersecurity practices.

The book covers essential cybersecurity topics, such as general cybersecurity tips, password protection, multi-factor identification, data encryption, and phishing attacks. The dark web also poses a significant threat to law firms, and I will show you how to use dark web monitoring tools to detect potential threats.

Additionally, the book emphasizes the importance of creating a culture of security in the workplace and ensuring employees are adequately trained. With these tips, law firms can protect their data, stay compliant with the latest regulations, and mitigate potential damages. However, it's important to note that this book is not a comprehensive solution to all your cybersecurity needs. It is a great resource that provides easy-to-implement tips and practical advice to help strengthen your law firm's cybersecurity posture, but it's not a panacea.

The book is written in a simple and easy-to-read format that anyone, from a partner to an intern, can learn from and implement. My goal is to make cybersecurity fun and accessible to everyone.

I hope you find this book informative and enjoyable.

Warm regards,

Tom Lambotte
Founder & CEO

INTRODUCTION

A DAY IN THE LIFE
OF A CYBERCRIMINAL

MORNING

You wake up at 6am and get ready for work. With a fresh cup of joe in one hand and remote control in the other, you turn on the tube — soaking in today's top news headlines. Your job depends on staying up to date; leveraging current events helps you connect with your prospects.

You hop on Zoom for your 8:30am virtual "stand-up" meeting, where the team reviews the day's tasks, goals, and performance expectations. The newest team member is welcomed, but you're a bit unimpressed. His specialty is social media trolling, which isn't really your thing. That being said, it is "in" right now, and he seems to have a good attitude; you can't help but recall your first day on the job here. The boss says the numbers are good but slipping a little, and it's crucial for the team to pick up the intensity a bit to hit this month's goals.

AFTERNOON

Given your past success, your boss assigned you the Business Email Compromise (BEC) gig this quarter, specifically focusing on wire fraud. Your goal for the quarter is to close five of these deals.

These are lucrative — averaging about $63,000 per occurrence and can run as high as $1 million. The job is to leverage dark web data to create very targeted emails, BEC scams, where you impersonate key company executives to trick employees into carrying out your requests — specifically to transfer funds to your bank account under the guise of being one of their colleagues.

This is one of the more people-centered roles since it takes gathering info from the dark web and researching the individuals via their website, LinkedIn, and news articles to look for relevant data points. From there, it is simply determination, persistence, and, ultimately, a numbers game. Your organization has a reputation to uphold, so you get to work.

New updates to corporate firewalls have made it a supreme hassle to break into a law firm's in-house server, so this approach is far easier. The best part? Even highly secured networks have no protection against this specific attack, since there's no attempt to access a computer or network.

EVENING

5pm rolls around, and you call it a day on the Business Email Compromise gig. Your brain's fried; while it is not very difficult work, it takes a lot of focus and energy to do it well. To dig and find the info that other more novice hackers tend to overlook.

Lying in bed, you check your email before calling it a night and smile ear-to-ear. A law firm's intern gave you his work email password. There's an open door to walk into tomorrow! A successful day's work! Easy, peasy. Rinse, lather, repeat.

CYBERSECURITY IN THE LEGAL FIELD DEMANDS PROACTIVE DILIGENCE

I characterize cybercrime this way to make a point. In the legal world, staying proactive – not reactive – to cybersecurity is how to combat organized, persistent online threats.

Cybercriminals don't wear black hoodies and live in dank, shady basements. They don't work in isolation and are not bored geeky high school kids with too much time on their hands. Real cyber criminals operate in an organized fashion. They are "real" businesses, just like yours and mine. They have company goals, key objectives, different roles on the team, and metrics to hit. They use the same business methodologies as we do to run efficient and profitable businesses. This level of organization allows them to make over six figures a year scamming people. If the thieves and fraudsters have a concerted, well-thought plan, shouldn't your cybersecurity practices be equally thorough? I hope you answered with a resoundingly loud yes! This hypothetical day in the life of a cybercriminal is not far from reality. Why don't you implement the security measures that would drastically reduce your likelihood of experiencing a data breach?

- Too busy to research all the options.
- Overwhelmed by options and choices.
- What do you really need?
- How much is too much? How much is too little?
- Is this just something being sold by the cybersecurity company making the product? Are they just scaremongering me into buying?

Ultimately, when faced with too many choices, most choose inaction. "I'll get to it one day." But that day never comes. You justify that when you get bigger, you will do something about it. You think things like "I'm just so busy, I don't have the time." And, "Cybercriminals don't care about mid-sized firms; they will go after the big guys." But you are wrong. I have seen many firms experience a data breach, and I can tell you firsthand that it is a terrible event to go through. And it's one that can be avoided with the right tools.

After nearly two decades of experience implementing comprehensive IT and cybersecurity for law firms, I wanted to write a book to help you find easy ways to take the first step in protecting your firm. Follow these tips and you are well on your way to making your firm much more difficult for cybercriminals to breach.

And, of course, if you need professional assistance to create the best defense against cybercriminals, the BobaGuard security suite provides comprehensive coverage in a turnkey solution. Most law firms lack the time and expertise to research and develop a proper security strategy that will cover you from all angles, so we built it for you. If you are interested in a free review of your current cybersecurity plan and how it can be improved, book a strategy call with one of our knowledgeable cybersecurity advisors at **www.bobaguard.com/strategy** to see how we can protect your firm from the bad guys.

GENERAL CYBERSECURITY

TIP #1:

THE IMPORTANCE
OF CYBERSECURITY

Staying abreast of cybersecurity is daunting to any tech layperson; it's not nearly as natural as locking a door, but equally important.

None of us would go to bed with our homes left unsecured – they hold our most private and precious possessions. Meanwhile, computers are practically virtual dwellings (I spend more time on my computer than my mattress) and are filled with 97% of your law firm's information (there are always those few unscanned files and legal pads). With all that information up for grabs to cybercriminals, it's no wonder that 1 in 4 law firms experienced a data breach.

Even worse, the Internet's mixed blessing of universal connectivity means that no matter where you live in the real world, online you permanently reside in the worst part of town, with invisible thieves living next door.

And that means your computer, loaded with your client's data — is at a potential risk of damaging your reputation, creating financial loss, and possible legal liability if you get hacked.

Practicing law means demonstrating an ethical commitment to client confidentiality, and you would never knowingly betray that trust, but a simple lapse in cybersecurity could undermine your best intentions.

Are you frightened yet?

I am — and I'm the expert!

Fortunately, cybersecurity — like home security — can be beefed up with the proper security layers.

Start with the basics. Take the time to research some simple strategies and protocols, then, even better, enlist a professional to review your measures and provide additional tools to monitor your infrastructure or make suggestions.

Cybersecurity is critical, but you don't need to live scared or be an expert — just be attentive, as any good homeowner would.

Remember: good fences make good neighbors around your lawn or your laptop.

TIP #2:

SECURE THE SCREEN — DON'T LET YOUR DATA WALK AWAY UNLOCKED

HERE'S A SCENE:

"I was working on my laptop in a shared workspace when nature called. I got up to use the bathroom, leaving the computer unattended. Although I was only gone for a couple of minutes, I discovered my account had been hacked the next day. What happened?"

DON'T MAKE THIS MISTAKE

The mistake? Not locking your computer screen. This scary reality is true for laptops and mobile devices alike, so screen locking is vital.

WHY PUTTING YOUR COMPUTER TO SLEEP ISN'T ENOUGH

Keep in mind that this tactic is far different from putting the computer to sleep. Confidential data is in jeopardy if anyone could click a button or swipe on the trackpad to access the desktop. Screen locking means requiring a password or PIN to get into the device. This simple strategy can be invaluable. I like to say that the things that are easy to do are also easy not to do.

HOW TO LOCK YOUR SCREEN

Fortunately, screen locking is also super simple.

On Mac:

» All you have to do is click on the Apple icon and select "lock screen."

» Or if you don't have a mouse handy, follow these steps:

» Press command + control + Q to do the same thing.

» If you've got a Mac equipped with the TouchBar, you can add a dedicated button for locking your Mac.

» Head to System Preferences > Keyboard, then click the "Customize Control Strip" button. Drag the Lock Screen button off the bottom of your screen and onto your Touchbar.

On PC:

» Press Ctrl + Alt + Del at the same time.

» Then select Lock from the options that appear.

» Alternatively, you can also do the following:

» Press the Windows logo on your keyboard + L at the same time.

FINAL THOUGHT

Now with a click of a button, your laptop is locked. So, pick one and use the bathroom in peace.

THREE WAYS TO PREVENT CYBER BREACHES AT THE OFFICE

Does the thought of a data breach send shivers down your spine? It does mine, too.

The rising incidence of data breaches and cybercrime is alarming, and we all must realize it's not just the big firms that are going down. Cybercriminals know the volume and type of sensitive information law firms are entrusted with. This makes law firms an attractive target for them.

In fact, a recent Legal Technology Survey from the American Bar Association found that 27% of responders reported that their law firms had experienced a security breach.

The more worrying statistic shows: 19% reported that they do not know whether their firm has ever experienced a security breach!

The good news is that you can reduce your risk by taking a few proactive steps. Case in point, we'll cover three ways you can prevent cyber breaches at the office.

1. TRAIN YOUR PEOPLE

The people who make your business operate are at once your first line of defense and one of your greatest liabilities. Train them to recognize the signs of phishing attacks, practice good password hygiene, and more.

2. TECH MATTERS

Your people are the first line of defense, but you need a backup. Cybersecurity technology like firewalls and malware detection software adds another layer of protection against intruders and other threats.

3. FILTER IT

Emails and web filters provide protection if (ahem, *when*) someone makes a mistake and errantly clicks on a suspicious link or ends up on a malicious website. Yes, they limit online access, but they deliver critical protection you can't do without.

There you go, three simple steps to prevent cyber breaches. Get to it.

TIP #4:

LIFE'S A BREACH —
SECURING EXTERNAL ACCOUNTS FROM
DATA BREACHES

Once more unto the breach, dear friends.

Our last tip provided simple steps to guard against breaches of your internal data, but responsibilities to your firm and your clients do not end at the local firewall.

With so much of your practice's legal, financial and privileged information stored in the cloud or shared with vendors whose security protocols are beyond your control, it's equally important to optimize data protection when it resides outside of your network.

Take a minute to consider all of the remote services employed in managing your cases and business: file sharing/storage, discovery review platforms, IT providers, banking, bookkeeping, and marketing partners — each possessing critical, private data from your firm and/or clients.

Now spend a few painful seconds considering how screwed (technical term) you'd be if any of them were hacked.

If you dare, imagine the potential cascading catastrophes resulting from exploiting credentials gathered in those breaches. Yikes!

OK, OK — take a deep breath and steel your resolve; even if you can't personally protect the integrity of these remote networks, there are several simple precautions to secure these accounts.

THESE INCLUDE:
- Always using unique passwords.
- Enabling two-factor authentication on all possible accounts.
- Vigilantly updating software and exorcising malware.
- Adhering to safe browsing practices.

These aren't too hard to employ, and it's 100% worth it to keep data safe, even on external accounts.

TIP #5:

IDENTITY THEFT — DON'T LET SOMEONE ELSE TAKE YOUR NAME IN VAIN

So many of us only consider security once it's too late.

Whether in business or personal life, identity theft is a unique nightmare worth trying to avoid.

Here are a few bad things that bad people can do with your ID information:

- Apply for credit cards or loans in your name.
- Withdraw funds from your bank account.
- Obtain medical care using your health insurance.
- Steal your tax refund using your social security number.
- Sell your information to other criminals.
- Conduct fraud by creating fake social media profiles with your name and photo.

- Blackmail you if they have sensitive information that could damage your public reputation.

These are the most common reasons why identity theft happens:

- Entering information on phishing websites that mimic the real thing (like a fake Facebook website).
- Not using up-to-date security software.
- Buying products from shady websites.
- Using public WiFi.
- Unsecure router.
- Using weak login credentials.
- Using the same login credentials in many places.
- Having weak privacy settings on social media.

If you can avoid making these mistakes, it will be much harder for criminals to get a hold of your identity and run havoc on your business. This week's post is more just a "what not to do".

See that list up above. Don't do it — lesson over.

Could it be any easier?

TIP #6:

THE BEST DEFENSE
IS A GREAT OFFENSE

True cybersecurity isn't about limiting damage, but preventing breaches and losses from occurring in the first place. With the right strategy and professionals in place, you can shed fear and focus instead on your firm.

There's no magic wand to banish the bad guys; it takes layers of overlapping protection: insulation, education, monitoring, and contingencies are all mission-critical components. Make sure your law firm's security stack includes each one.

Insulation

Integrated password management automatically ensures (and securely stores) unique passwords that isolate compromised credentials, while implementing multi-factor authentication quickly retires leaked passwords.

Education

Humans are the weakest link in any cybersecurity plan, and today's sophisticated phishing and fraud tactics make it crucial to keep staff on their toes. Training programs should be interesting enough to retain attention, spaced apart so they aren't ignored, and backed by unannounced simulations to verify lessons have been learned.

Monitoring

An initial audit identifies existing weak spots, and regular risk assessments keep everything fine-tuned. Proactive probing, coupled with testing and installing security updates, helps defeat emerging new threats. Regularly scanning the dark web keeps tabs on credentials to ensure your identity remains safe.

Contingencies

It's impossible to guarantee absolute protection, so any realistic approach prepares for problems. Established security protocols should provide guidance in case of a breach; while offsite data backups keep your files secure and cyber insurance shields you from liability.

Cybersecurity threats aren't simple, and neither are defenses against them. It's true there's no magic wand of protection, but luckily there are steps you can take to keep your personal and professional data safe. To make it even easier for you, we've created a Cybersecurity Checklist for Busy Lawyers that you can download here: **www.bobaguard.com/SSSTChecklist** to see how your firm is faring when it comes to being cybersecure.

PASSWORDS & ENCRYPTION

TALES FROM THE ENCRYPT

We're not entirely done optimizing your protection — here is another crucial (but easy and FREE!) step towards avoiding catastrophic computer consequences.

You've worked on securing internal and external accounts and even used a VPN to connect your laptop at Starbucks. Great job! You've made significant progress in covering your cybersecurity bases and deserve to celebrate with a caramel macchiato with extra whipped cream! But when you get back to the table, your laptop is gone.

Shoot.

We get so focused online that it's easy to neglect real life, forgetting the threat isn't just hackers but thieves. Worse yet, if the crooks are tech-savvy, they can access your data and own your hard drive in under 10 minutes.

Luckily there's a simple proactive measure to protect against such intrusion, and it's already built into your computer: full disk encryption (FDE).

Your old startup screen might've kept your niece out of your browsing history but was easily defeated by professionals, whereas FDE (using pre-boot biometric locks and/or a separate PIN) encrypts everything on your hard drive, rendering your device useless to anyone but you.

Best of all, FDE is already installed on your Mac (via FileVault) or Windows 10 device (via BitLocker) — so please ensure that is enabled!

ON A MAC
» Navigate to "System Settings"
» Scroll to "Privacy & Security"
» Confirm that "FileVault" is turned on and if not, enable it now.

ON A PC
On Windows 10, simply search your settings for "Device Encryption" and verify that it's turned on.

» Choose "Start" and then go to "Settings".
» Select "Privacy and Security", and then go to "Device encryption".
» If Device encryption is turned off, turn it to on.

UNRAVELING THE DATA

Most new machines enable encryption by default, but a recent ABA tech survey revealed that only 22% of attorneys were using it: take a minute right now to make sure that you are one of the smart ones.

Don't forget that if you lose both your account password and your recovery key, you won't be able to log in to your computer or access the data on your startup disk. Always store your recovery key securely; we always recommend a password manager.

Maybe we can't stop thieves or prevent careless misplacement, but with full disk encryption, you can buy some peace of mind while protecting yourself, your data, and your clients from a worst-case scenario.

Ok, now you can enjoy that coffee.

TIP #8

DISABLE YOUR AUTOMATIC LOGIN

Your future self will thank you for this tip.

We know it's easier to log in automatically to your computer every time you start, but that makes it just as easy for thieves and hackers if you misplace your laptop.

The odds are extremely low that, on your laptop, you have automatic login enabled, thanks to security improvements that computer companies have made.

And, hopefully, you previously turned your encryption on already, so you are prompted to enter your password upon logging in each time you access your computer.

Let's take a minute and double-check to be certain.

Remember, these tips only help you when you implement them, which is always the most challenging part.

If you haven't already, here's how to disable your automatic login:

ON A MAC
- Go to the Apple Menu.
- Go to "System Settings".
- Click on "Users and Groups".
- Switch the automatic login feature to "off" for all users on your Mac. You can also set advanced settings, like showing password hints.

ON A PC
1. Press "Win + R", and enter "netplwiz" opening the "User Accounts" window.
2. Check that the option for "Users must enter a username and password to use this computer" is selected and if not, check that box and select "Apply".
3. Restart your computer and you will be prompted to enter your password on the login screen.

Could it be any easier?

Make sure you pick a strong password (*not your birthday!*) and keep it somewhere safe in case you forget it.

TIP #9:

YOU GOTTA KEEP 'EM SEPARATED

I haven't always made the best choices when it's come to security over the years (like, pretty much everyone at one point or another).

One step I took early on was for both security and simplification. This was the choice to use different emails, usernames, and passwords for professional and private purposes. I have a personal email and my work email address. Different passwords for each.

Did you know that your email and password could be circulating online already? If you've used the same email address and password to sign into various forums and websites that aren't too secure, there's a risk that the security of at least one of those websites was breached and your data among that of many others stolen by hackers.

We know your odds are not in your favor since we have been offering a dark web scanning solution to our clients since 2018. Almost everyone has something out there already.

My personal email and password were on the dark web. And so was my wife's! Luckily, I changed the password before anything bad happened. I admit we both had used the same password and email address for logging in in many places.

This is why it's super important to separate your business emails and passwords from private ones. And, of course, try to use as many different emails and (long) passwords as you can to further minimize risks from security breaches.

TIP #10:

UNIQUE PASSWORDS

Of all the Stupid Simple Security Tips I will share, perhaps none is as simple — or as stupid to ignore as: **Always use unique passwords.**

Like brushing your teeth, filling your fuel tank, or saving up money for retirement, proper management of passwords can feel like thankless drudgery that's easy to skip but proves disastrous once negligence comes due.

Luckily there are now tools that will automatically diversify your passwords and keep track of them across your entire array of devices, making this critical measure easier than ever. Password managers can do a lot to provide and store unique passwords; however, you'll still need to brush your teeth.

To drive home this tip's importance, let's take a quick look at why it's crucial to compartmentalize account access.

Homo sapiens are creatures of habit who, by default, use only a few passwords. Most people have a basic go-to password that is easy to remember. Perhaps something like a beloved pet's name. When some website calls out our weak sauce, we reluctantly add on our spouse's birthday. Encountering even higher security, we're prompted to include alternate cases and symbols, so we capitalize the pet name, toss on a question mark, and feel invincible to any army of hackers. Peaches1215? Forever!

We carry on using and reusing these same three passwords until there comes news of a breach.

Still, we don't bat an eye about Netflix's compromised data — we're not ashamed of binging Bridgerton! Of course, the problem is that those credentials are now for sale on the dark web, and any place you access with your email and a repeated password is now vulnerable to exploitation.

To do nothing would be tantamount to learning that your house keys had been copied all over town but failing to call up a locksmith to change the locks.

So, what should we do?

Rather than buying a new pet or supplementing passwords with a fresh slew of question marks tracked by an endless succession of Post-It notes, get a password manager to generate and store unique keys for all your accounts.

Several good products are on the market – from subscription services to apps to browser extensions. The best software will generate unique long-string passwords on demand, save them securely in the cloud for cross-platform retrieval, associate them by domain, and even auto-fill them upon verification – no memory or mess required.

After choosing a manager, immediately visit the ten most critical accounts you use daily and replace your passwords. (Pretend ALL your accounts have been breached. Which ten would stress you out the most?) Eventually, you should update the rest on a rolling basis as you access them. It's a bit of a pain, but a one-time task that could prove invaluable in the long run.

Don't be stupid; take this simple tip – and rest easier knowing you're far more secure.

Please!

TIP #11:

ARE YOUR PASSWORDS SAFE?

Keeping your accounts and personal information secure has become more critical than ever before. With the rise of cybercrimes, hackers are looking for new ways to access personal information such as credit card numbers, social security numbers, and email usernames. Luckily there are plenty of ways to protect ourselves from criminals while still using the internet and technology.

First, we want to start by ensuring we aren't using easy-to-guess passwords, so whenever possible, go for length. Old advice said to use special characters to replace letters and numbers. Even more effective is to focus on length by selecting three unrelated words. When creating passwords, the longer it is, the more secure it is.

In addition to not choosing an obvious password, using different passwords for each of your online accounts is also good. This way, even if one of the sites you're using is compromised by hackers, they can't access all your accounts because they would have to guess multiple passwords.

In truth, the best passwords are those you don't need to remember at all. For this reason, we usually strongly recommend that people use password managers. These easy-to-use tools will create very complex passwords you don't even have to remember. In addition, they help you to manage multiple passwords, secure notes, credit cards, and other personal details. The application will generate strong passwords for each of the accounts you have and store them behind one master password. This makes it much easier to keep track of your online accounts and their corresponding usernames/passwords.

There are many different options for password managers. Some of the most popular ones are Dashlane, LastPass, Roboform, SplashID, 1Password, and KeePass. It's important to note that no matter what type of password manager you use, it will not protect you from hackers who can obtain your personal information through keyloggers or phishing scams, so it's always good to take the necessary precautions when surfing the web. These include using security software on your computer and browsing reputable and secure websites. By following these simple guidelines, you can keep your passwords safe while enjoying all that technology offers.

And for an easy-to-use reference guide, we've created this free download of password best practices to utilize. Use this link: **www.bobaguard.com/SSSTpassword** to download a copy for your firm.

BE AWARE OF THE WEAKEST LINK

If you're reading this, there's a good chance you have one or more work and online accounts where passwords are required. (Duh, right?)

A recent study revealed that the average person has 30 passwords to remember. I think that is shockingly low. I have over 982 logins in my password manager. Given this, it's no surprise that people are tempted to use the same password for many different accounts.

Passwords are a form of security to identify people and secure their identities and data.

They've grown so popular; it's difficult to imagine life without them. They're everywhere — from computers to smartphones to bank accounts, video games, and social media — and they serve as the foundation for many other technologies.

Despite all the progress in computer technology, employees remain the weakest link in the security chain. User blunders often negate any effective security policy. According to studies, compromised email is the most prevalent means of stealing user accounts.

Consider how crucial a firm's strong password policy is to its success.

A close friend of mine, who also runs an IT company, recently shared a story his client experienced with me. His client called him, concerned about a possible email hack at their firm. On the closing day, one of their lawyers got an email from a client conducting a mortgage close. The email came from the customer's correct electronic mail address and was correctly addressed to the attorney. It simply required that he wire the cash to their bank after completing the funding.

All the required information was included in the email, including the routing instructions and account information for their new bank.

As you probably guessed, the closing attorney transmitted $650,000 to the wrong bank.

Did they have a procedure to double-check the bank account data that arrived by email? Yes, they did, but the attorney ignored the proper steps. (That's a different lesson.) The money was stolen as a result. This is, unfortunately, all too typical of an occurrence.

How does this relate to password security, you might ask? The closing attorney's email was not hacked. On the other hand, his client's email account was and is the topic of this lesson.

Law firms that follow best practices for password security often neglect them for personal accounts, particularly personal email accounts.

It was not his client's email account that had been hacked, but a client of his client. The more sophisticated hackers do not spam you or send hundreds of emails to everyone in the account's contacts list. Nor do they leave any indications that they are reading your emails. They lurk, read, and wait for their chance. That is precisely what occurred in this example.

Don't forget how convenient the indexing works in your email provider. Whether 365 or G-Workspace, anyone in your account can run searches to get to the good stuff immediately:

- Routing number
- Password
- Bank info
- SSN
- Social security number

Any clever criminal will have a list of the top 10 keyword searches to get them to the juiciest info stored within email accounts. Then they get to work.

Most of us don't realize that our emails are potentially being read by skilled hackers every day. A seasoned hacker may get a comprehensive picture of your life if they gain access to your email. Or do the same for one of your team members. Someone spending a week reading through our email history would discover your banking, investing, childcare, business, and shopping habits, as well as private communications between colleagues, friends and family members.

If this makes you uncomfortable, I'm relieved. Hopefully, it will push you to add preventative cybersecurity measures to protect your firm before a well-planned email message is received from your friendly neighborhood hacker!

For all law firms, from small to large, password security is — or at least should be — an essential component of your overall security plan. Any policy you develop or modify should aid in the prevention of guessing one's passwords, along with other advanced password attacks.

TIP #13:
2FA OR NOT 2FA,
THAT IS THE QUESTION

We've established the importance of securing online access and the need to employ unique passwords. Still, password protection alone isn't enough — you should enable another critical layer of verification with any restricted account. The bad news is that only 39% of lawyers are making use of this, according to a recent ABA TechReport. The good news is that this additional security is already built into almost every online portal. The only thing you need to do is turn it on.

You've likely already been asked to enable Two-factor Authentication (2FA) and skipped it out of convenience or unfamiliarity. Let's address the excuse I hear the most and rectify it. The most common reason is, "But it's more work to sign in, and it's annoying." Let me ask you this: What is more annoying, taking a few seconds when logging in or dealing with a data breach? Fact: your critical accounts are under attack. The bad guys really want to get in. Choose your own adventure here, do you:

- Ignore it, cross your fingers, and hope for the best and NOT enable a free security layer that would drastically increase the security of your practice.

OR

- Take a few minutes to set it up, educate your team on the why and how, and significantly increase your data safety by enabling this additional security layer.

One more scenario. Let's pretend you suffered a data breach and are now answering to an ethics committee as to why you didn't have 2FA enabled. How sympathetic would they feel to your response: "It was annoying?"

Consider this: If a site you use only requires a password to get in and doesn't offer 2FA, there's a good chance that it will eventually be hacked. 2FA is an extra layer of security to ensure that people trying to gain access to an online account are who they say they are. First, a user will enter their username and password. Then, instead of immediately gaining access, they will be required to provide another piece of information (that's the 2FA — Two-Factor Authentication).

There are many options for 2FA, like a secondary pin to a physical possession (key fob that generates a token) to personal security questions, GPS location, biometric signatures, or access to an independent account (SMS/email — another reason to use different passwords!).

What I want you to take away from today is that the overwhelming majority of your online accounts should have 2FA available, and you should take the time to set this up. Commit to setting this up on the ten prime accounts where you already replaced your passwords and ensure that 2FA is enabled. There should be a link on the access screen (if not, check the help section, Google it, or call the institution). Confirmation will take just a minute and likely won't be necessary with every log-in, usually only after a prolonged absence or when you sign in from new devices or locations. You're safer already!

Never think of the second factor as an inconvenience that takes all of 12 seconds, but a layer of comfort that brings peace of mind. And please don't ever tell me "it's annoying so I don't use it" — that's a sore spot for me. Imagine if you said that about locking your car door; "Yeah, well, I would have locked my car, but I would have had to open my bag, take my keys out, press the buttons, just too much work." It takes slightly more work to set up, but it significantly increases security and peace of mind.

TIP #14:

A HACKER'S NUMBER ONE METHOD

A weak password is still the number one method hackers use to gain access to your data.

Recent data shows that 81% of hacking-related breaches leveraged either stolen and/or weak passwords.

Did you know 59% of people reuse their passwords everywhere, both at work and home?

Here's a recipe for building strong passwords:

- A minimum of eight characters — the longer a password is, the more secure it is. A great way to get there is to **take three unrelated words and add a special character to separate them.**

- Use both UPPERCASE and lowercase letters.
- At least one number and one symbol (#, for example).
- Don't use a single, complete word by itself, like "PaSsWord123#". While this meets the requirements, a hacker's brute-force software will crack that in seconds.
- Never reuse a password for multiple accounts (like making your Facebook and LinkedIn passwords the same).

Education and safe password practices should be a top priority for everyone on your team to protect your firm from cybercriminals looking to infiltrate your data.

Requiring the use of a password manager also helps to eliminate the use of weak passwords.

A password policy should be implemented and signed by all firm members to ensure everyone knows and will follow the above guidelines.

Putting these practices into place will build the defense to protect your data from cybercriminals.

MULTI-FACTOR AUTHENTICATION OR PASSWORD MANAGER? HOW TO CHOOSE?

For any law firm, password security is (or at least should be) an essential component of your overall security plan. Any policy you develop or modify should aid in the prevention of guessing one's passwords, along with other advanced password attacks.

Today, most password management apps aid you in establishing and enforcing strong password requirements.

Passwords should be at least eight characters long and include a combination of letters and symbols. Passwords should not be recycled, and enforcement to prevent workers from reusing their original passwords for their applications should be a part of any good password management policy. And that's the bare minimum.

However, too many law firms (especially small and mid-sized) fall into the trap of using (and reusing) insecure passwords rather than utilizing the tools at their disposal. They neglect to enforce basic standards on every worker's computer and logins, particularly email accounts.

I'm still shocked at how many law firms put convenience ahead of security, especially when it comes to email passwords. Changing your email password, synchronizing it across all your devices, and enabling 2FA may be difficult, especially since email has become essential to our job and personal lives.

How do you apply a password policy incorporating all the sophisticated recommendations while knowing you still need to remember these passwords? We've got to be able to keep them straight without writing them down on a sticky note.

Two of the best solutions to this problem are multi-factor authentication and password management apps.

The key question is: how can you and your employees safely access critical systems requiring passwords while maintaining password security procedures?

Multi-factor Authentication (MFA) is one of the most cost-effective ways for law firms to secure digital assets. As more businesses migrate their valuable data and servers to the cloud, two-factor or multi-factor authentication has gone from a "should probably do" to an "absolutely must-have." In basic terms, multi-factor or two-factor authentication adds another layer of security to your login procedure.

Users must authenticate using a second means in addition to the conventional username and password. Verifying a previously chosen picture or personal data is one example of establishing a secure connection before logging into sensitive locations. A one-time password or pin delivered to the user's mobile phone via text falls within the simple category. An advanced method uses a token app or card with a rolling pin that changes regularly.

The usage of password managers is the next must-have. Password managers store your login information for all the apps and websites you use, allowing you to generate and safely store many passwords. Most of them can automatically log you into the apps and websites, making the experience of creating unique, secure passwords and logging into websites effortless.

The goal of a password manager is to encrypt your password database and store it in an encrypted manner. The only password you must remember is the one used to access the password manager.

Passwords are now managed and controlled from a single location, making this service ideal for businesses. Your firm may take advantage of this service with a program that utilizes sharing and managing individual and system passwords from a centrally maintained platform.

The top of these systems provides cross-platform compatibility (Mac, Windows, and Mobile), multi-factor authentication, biometrics in the iPhone and iOS, and regular password audits that help identify weak and duplicate passwords and rank users' security posture.

It is not my goal to scare you, but to create greater awareness. After reading this, you may conclude that having stringent password policies in place is just too much of a hassle. I hope it's not the case, but if so, please realize how critical secure password security is to your firm's security.

PHISHING

USE YOUR NOGGIN'

Improved passwords and two-factor authentication have made you a safer visitor while blocking malware has helped secure your home turf, but how do you protect yourself in-between while browsing the wild, wild west of the World Wide Web? (Try saying that ten times fast)!

You can take several simple steps to avoid evil on the Internet, and most boil down to using your brain and taking precautions.

THINK SMART

Don't be foolish while browsing — be aware!

Specifically, beware of phishing scams designed to trick you into surrendering credentials on spoofed pages posing as legitimate sites.

Simple hoaxes that began with "princes" needing urgent help and access to your bank accounts have evolved into sophisticated rackets which convincingly mimic reputable institutions. Still, if you're smart about it, you'll be safe.

Before surrendering sensitive information, always consider the source, the request, and the location.

- If you receive an uncharacteristic message from any source, ask yourself, "Why am I getting this? Did I request this? Does this seem right?"
- Remember that no trustworthy company will ever solicit sensitive information (including passwords) via email.
- Before submitting credentials to any website, confirm your browser's address bar contains a lock icon indicating a secure, certified connection (scammers often use URLs that are deceptively close to the sites they're spoofing).

In fact, a good rule of thumb is never to follow an email link to a secure site — use a bookmark or search engine to ensure you're at the genuine site, double-check for the lock, and navigate from there.

AN OUNCE OF PREVENTION

How does the Secret Service protect the President between secure locations? They use a bulletproof car. How do you hire a bulletproof car for the information superhighway? You use a VPN.

Virtual Private Networks are the perfect prophylactic whenever using public Wi-Fi (airports, coffee shops, workspaces, etc.). These subscription services act like portable firewalls, accessed via apps that provide end-to-end encryption to keep bad guys from eyeing your traffic or grabbing your info out of the air.

There are many good VPNs available for a few bucks a month — always employ them on unsecured connections, and there's no harm in using them while on a trusted network (the safest bet is to set them to always be on).

LAST THOUGHTS

A little common sense and a little technology can keep you safe when browsing; be smart with your data and secure with your connections (while educating employees to do the same) and your information will safe and sound.

TIP #17:

GONE PHISHING

Of the countless threats to data security, one of the most widespread and successful is also one of the simplest: phishing.

Phishing is a fraud that exploits human frailty rather than technological weak points and has thrived in the era of constantly being online. While IT tools can limit phishing exposure and mitigate damages, the most effective defense is awareness — so let me drop some knowledge that might keep you safe.

WHAT IS PHISHING?

Phishing scams use emails disguised as legitimate requests to extract info or bypass security. Digital con artists pose as trusted contacts who direct you to click links, download files, or submit credentials that are then used to attack related accounts and systems.

The "con" in "con artist" is short for "confidence," and that's just what these tricksters use against you – sending messages crafted to seem genuine with logos, language, and links that lower your guard and suspicion.

Messages might pretend to be an email provider, employer, bank, utility service provider, or an app/social network urgently asking you to confirm your personal information, but are actually traps waiting to install malware, ransomware, or steal your passwords.

DON'T TAKE THE BAIT!

Sophisticated email filters and updated software will thwart some attempts. Proper password management, data encryption, and file backups can temper catastrophes after the fact, but the main line of defense against phishing is YOU!

These attacks are passive and don't work without your compliance, so it's critical that you learn to discern phishing messages and defer to your Spidey Senses if anything seems suspicious.

Three crucial tools can protect you from phishing emails.

1.   Consistent cybersecurity training.
2.   Simulated phishing emails to test your acumen.
3.   Self-learning email security platforms designed to detect nefarious emails slipping through traditional anti-phishing defenses quickly.

The most common advice when assessing suspicious messages is to **pause before clicking**.

Any requests that feel odd or out-of-the-ordinary should be scrutinized through cynical eyes:

- Is the sender known?
- Did they address you personally?
- Is the branding off?
- Is the language/spelling/tone professional?
- Is a request unusual?
- Are the URLs clean, or do they contain extra characters (and do links look the same when you hover over them)?

If you doubt any of these aspects, find a secure way to verify the communication.

Phishing fraud has become so sophisticated and spoof websites so tricky to spot that my advice these days is just don't click! If a vendor or service provider needs information, they will also post it to your account. Rather than following a link or freely submitting info via email, follow your usual channel to log in and check for messages securely. If it's a friend or an employer reaching out, write them separately instead of simply hitting "reply."

KEEPING IT REEL

Often when I lecture on phishing, I'm met with resistance from folks that say, "I'd never fall for that!" but you'd be surprised. Tech titans like Facebook and Google, major corporations, and governmental agencies have succumbed to such attacks. All it takes is one slip-up by a single employee during a busy day, and all your data (or dollars) could be compromised or lost.

Updating system security offers a layer of protection, but with phishing, the best defense is education. All staff members from the top-down need to have regular phishing education to know what to look out for as phishing continues to grow in sophistication. And be wary of any IT advisor who ignores the human element.

TIP #18:

BAIT SHOP — GOOGLE DOCS

Phishing is one of cybersecurity's most serious threats and the one most preventable by users. Knowing what to look for can steer you clear of these traps that target your network and identity.

Since awareness is your best defense against phishing scams, this tip is focused on a dangerous scam that uses our reliance on Google Docs.

Google Docs is a popular platform run by a trusted tech giant, which is precisely what makes it perfect for phishing. Invoking Google's good name earns the targets' trust, while hackers who reach out from Google's system can avoid email filters designed to detect them.

So, this phishing bait uses HTML trickery to squat in a supposedly safe space while camouflaged to blend in perfectly; it's like a stick bug if stick bugs were deadly!

The scam plays out like this: you receive a legitimate Google Docs invite linked to an actual Google Docs file location, where instead of the expected file, you encounter an HTML insert that mimics the platform's appearance while prompting one more click.

That coded "download" link instead redirects you to a phishing site that requests your credentials to proceed.

You believe you're verifying an account but have just given the bad guys your password. Game. Set. Match.

Like so many phishing attacks, it's easy to fall for, which is why you must remain hyper-vigilant. There are two things to remember:

1. ALWAYS THINK BEFORE YOU CLICK

If you receive a Google Doc invitation, take a moment to assess whether it was expected, who actually sent it, and what client/case it supposedly involves. If something smells "phishy," seek confirmation.

2. ALWAYS TRIPLE-CHECK BEFORE SUBMITTING CREDENTIALS

When asked for a password, ensure you're connected to the expected domain with a verified "lock" symbol in the address bar. Better yet, never submit a password on a landing page;

instead, access the page/account independently through the host's authentic URL.

Phishing attacks have become crazily sophisticated, and keeping your data safe requires sharp eyes. Ideally, your team should be protected by the latest security tools and awareness training, but at least be careful and remember that hackers can be disguised as anyone.

Don't take the bait!

TIP #19:

THE LANGUAGE OF LIES

Email scams are in our mailboxes daily and continue to surge, with recent data suggesting phishing attacks rose 61% in one year. Instead of stressing the consequences of inaction or tech countermeasures, this tip focuses on the language of lies these "phishermen" spin. A recent analysis covering thousands of bogus emails has identified their most prominent go-to words and phrases, letting us study the vocabulary of these scammers for better detection.

Phishing attacks trick us into actions that undermine our security: clicking on links, downloading code, or changing settings to make us more vulnerable. As the deceptive messages must seem legitimate to avoid suspicion, they aim to mimic recognized senders. That's why the best ones are tough to spot — they're crafted like everything else in your mailbox. Yet even sophisticated phishing attacks are still scams at their core and rely upon recognizable tactics. Hackers use a variety of methods to win our trust. They'll often start by impersonating a known contact (even spoofing web addresses and logos), then use subject lines that sound somewhat familiar. These subject lines will also include URGENT language, prompting us to open the message and complete some ACTION quickly. The specific words and phrases used will vary by context, but studies show they're most likely to fall into one of these categories:

PROFESSIONAL MESSAGES

Masquerading as messages from your employer, clients, or service providers, these attempts prey on the desire to be an attentive employee. Buzzwords include:

- IT Desk
- Documents
- Invoice
- Request
- Policy
- Follow-up
- Meeting
- File
- Action
- Urgent

SECURITY MESSAGES

These emails offer to help with protection (or alert you to hacking) while aiming to corrupt your system. Buzzwords include:

- Verify
- Reset
- Compromised
- Validate
- Suspicious
- Update
- Login
- Unauthorized
- Password
- Activity

HEADLINE MESSAGES

Using anxiety tied to the day's news, these emails tempt us with promises of important info. Buzzwords include:

- Ransomware
- Mandate
- IRS
- Taxes
- Bitcoin

PERSONAL MESSAGES

Hoping to interest us with social media activity or blend with online orders/interests, these messages often pretend to be from apps or retailers. Buzzwords include:

- Delivery
- Address
- Purchase
- Tagged
- Mentioned
- Refill
- Account
- Expired
- Balance

These buzzwords alone don't make an email phishy but should raise suspicion. More so when they're coupled with phrases that prompt quick action or accompanied by poor grammar and misspellings (many scams originate overseas with non-native speakers). Ironically, language can be either the camouflage that masks a convincing scam or the flaw that gives it away! When in doubt

1) Don't click on anything.

2) Close the email.

3) Independently navigate to verified domains.

SQUISH THE SMISH

Smish.

Smishing.

Smished.

I find it to be an annoying word in and of itself. However, today, we must talk about it.

Smishing is a technique in which hackers use a compelling text message to trick their victims into taking an unwanted action.

Hackers know people are more inclined to view and answer text messages than their emails quickly. Hackers can quickly convince someone to take action without thinking with their guard let down. The word smishing is a combination of Short

Message Service (SMS) and phishing. Both techniques are designed to send convincing messages to make you take an unwanted action: smishing via text message and phishing via email. It's easy for a hacker to look like someone else in a smishing attack. That's because most SMS messages are not authenticated and can be sent by anyone without the validation of the sender.

Not all smishing is delivered via a text message. With the variety of messaging apps on your phone, hackers have many choices they use to deliver their compelling tricks (such as Facebook Messenger). Don't reply to an unsolicited message since that will confirm your actual number, leaving you a target for additional attacks. If you get an unsolicited message, your first reaction should always be to stop and think if it's legit. Never give away PINs, passwords, or other sensitive information in response to a text or message on any app.

Smishing can be sent to anyone with a valid phone number. It's important to remember that your location doesn't matter if you're at work or at home to be a target of smishing. A smishing attack might ask you to call back a phone number or provide a pin or password to "confirm" your information. The best action is no action. Always verify directly with the service or person about its authenticity by calling the company using a number you have used before or emailing a contact you found on their website.

Certain smishing attacks focus on tricking you into giving up your multi-factor code. Again, the best action is no action, and consider changing your password if you believe it has been compromised. If you aren't sure if a text you have received is a smishing attack, don't hesitate to ask for help. You might not be the only one being targeted and can help prevent your peers from becoming victims.

DON'T CLICK LINKS

First, if there's a link in the message, don't click it. If you're concerned about the authenticity of a message, directly contact the service or person trying to interact with you.

DON'T RESPOND

When it comes to receiving a smish, the best action is no action. Responding to a smishing attack lets the hacker confirm you are engaged and gives them more opportunities to target you further.

TAKE A MOMENT

An unsolicited text message is going to look and feel urgent. Hackers want you to act before you think, which is why many smishing attacks are successful.

Smishing attacks rely on someone to engage with them to be effective. Help others in your organization learn how to spot and stop smishing at work and home.

TIP# 21:

TURN OFF YOUR BRAIN'S
AUTOPILOT FEATURE

I confess that even though I'm a cybersecurity expert, there are times throughout the day when I put my brain on autopilot. But who among us doesn't?

Unfortunately, while sliding our minds into self-driving mode has its advantages (for example, it lets us multitask better), it's also a risk-strewn practice.

It's risky because it can distract us from scrutinizing incoming emails for telltale signs of a phishing attack. And unless you're paying attention, you may mindlessly open baited emails and then hook-line-and-sinker, download their malware-laced attachments or click on their lethal links.

That's why you must turn off your brain's autonomous control mechanism when perusing emails. With yourself back behind the mental wheel (and your hands firmly gripping it at the 10 o'clock and 2 o'clock positions), you'll be more likely to spot these indicators of phishyness.

1. REQUESTS FOR CONFIDENTIAL PERSONAL OR FINANCIAL INFORMATION

My personal favorite is the one where the sender sheepishly confesses to having lost my Social Security number and would I please be a sport by "resupplying" it.

2. UNUSUAL "FROM" OR URL ADDRESSES

A real email from, say, your bank might have an address along the lines of "customer_service@yourbank.com" as opposed to "yourbank_customer_service@LOL.com" or "customer_service@yourbank.com/LOL_sucker."

3. ATTACHMENTS AND LINKS.

Never download or click email links without first confirming by phone to a trusted number via a reply to a confirmed valid email address that it was actually sent by an authorized sender. Tournament-level phishermen know how to counterfeit with stunning accuracy the appearance of emails from your family, friends, colleagues, and vendors.

4. MISSPELLINGS AND POOR GRAMMAR

Legitimate businesses and government entities rarely send emails containing language gaffes. Cybercrooks are far more eager to con you than to impress you with eloquence or dictionary skills.

Bottom line: phishing is a serious cyber threat to you and your firm, but you can defend against it.

GET TRAINED TO DETECT SPEAR PHISHING

Spear phishing attacks are like regular phishing attacks, only a lot more insidious.

An ordinary phishing attack usually involves sending out a spoof mass email that tries to trick a whole bunch of people into giving out their personal information or clicking a website link that dumps viruses and ransomware into your systems.

Spear phishing, however, tries to trick just one person — you.

Its generic nature makes ordinary phishing relatively easy to spot and dodge. For example, you receive an email from a name-brand bank frantically alerting you that your account has been compromised and advising you to log in via this "special" supplied link to reset your password. The problem is that you don't have an account with that bank. So, duh, obvious scam.

Not so obvious, however, is a spear phishing attack because it utilizes information relevant to you. For example, drawing on publicly available or illicitly procured details of your life, phishers can convincingly impersonate people in your circle to gain your trust and get you to do their ruinous bidding.

To tell whether an email purporting to be from people you know is legit or a trap, you (and your entire team, for that matter) should sign up for phishing detection training.

Plenty of training courses are available, but the best ones spread the instruction over multiple short lessons and use fun-infused storytelling techniques to memorably impart information (as opposed to a half-day or day-long seminar laced with dry, dull, and largely forgettable PowerPoint bullet-style presentations).

The most effective training programs also provide detection practice using actual spear phishing emails rather than hypothetical, lab-concocted examples.

Looking into spear phishing detection training is something you should put at the top of today's to-do list.

DON'T GO INTO THE UNKNOWN

As you know, roaming the internet can be a risky proposition. There are, for instance, trap websites awaiting your arrival so they can infect your computer with viruses, malware, ransomware, scripts, and other bad stuff. That's why you should avoid unfamiliar websites and visit only trustworthy ones.

But how do you determine the trustworthiness of a site you've never before visited?

Easy. First, hover your mouse over the link you're planning to click to take you to that site. The site's full URL — its internet address — will then become visible.

Check to see if the URL begins with the letters HTTPS.

That's computer shorthand for Hypertext Transfer Protocol Secure. It means the site's owner has obtained a Secure Sockets Layer (SSL) certificate, which gives assurance that the data you exchange with the website will be encrypted.

If you don't see HTTPS at the beginning of the URL, what might show up instead is HTTP (no "S" at the end). That means the site is unsecured, and the data you exchange will not be encrypted.

Suppose you go straight to a site (without first doing the mouse hover), and the URL in your browser's address bar is missing the HTTPS or even the HTTP prefix. You'll still be able to tell if the site has SSL certification. Just look for a little padlock icon in front of the URL. If you see it, you're golden.

Be mindful that neither HTTPS nor the padlock icon guarantees the site is legit. It could still be a trap. However, such risk is relatively low because cybercriminals typically hate getting SSL certification – the process requires too much effort and public exposure for their liking.

So stay away from unfamiliar sites. But if you visit them, you must then at least verify that they can encrypt the data you exchange.

THE DARK WEB

DARK WEB, DARKER NEWS

Put on your black hoodies; it's time to peek at the dark web, a nefarious presence that seems almost fictional but is the home to some very real threats.

You may not know what the dark web is, but that doesn't mean it's unaware of you — so arm yourself with a bit of knowledge and a quick lesson on how to stay safe.

The "Dark Web" refers to Internet areas that are neither indexed nor publicly available. Access requires special software, and its traffic is untraceable and anonymous. It isn't inherently illegal, but no one needs that kind of privacy to swap cookie recipes.

All manner of illicit activity can be found there. Still, the gravest threats to your law firm's security are phishing scam kits, marketplaces to swap stolen credentials, and ransomware attacks spawned by stolen data.

Dark web activity continues to surge, and the cybercrimes from this dark hole target everyone on the regular web and our assets in real life.

What can you do?

Besides precautions such as browsing safely, avoiding phishing scams, and limiting password exposure, there is only one truly effective way to fend off dark web threats and combat the commoditization of your data; you need someone to shine a light into shadowy corners and keep an eye on your info. This light of additional protection is called dark web monitoring, which continuously scans for compromised data from your domain(s) and lets your employees ensure the security of their identities and credentials. This proactive breach detection minimizes the damage as you will be quickly alerted as soon as any of your domains show up on the dark web, which is a sure sign that your information has been purloined. Once you are notified that you have credit on the dark web, take some time to immediately change any passwords or usernames for accounts that have been breached. This will keep you one step ahead of the cyber thieves!

DUDE, WHERE ARE MY CREDENTIALS?

Credential theft is the most common and costly of all cybercrimes, yet most don't understand the threat, and many don't even know when they've been victimized.

THE DANGER

Major data breaches occur so often that we've become numb to them as news. Nowadays, to make headlines, breaches often need well over 200 million accounts compromised! Failing to perceive the potential of personal exposure, we tend to tune out such stories.

"What's somebody gonna do with my Twitter account — post a lame meme?" they wryly ask. "So long as I change my Netflix password before they ruin my watch list, I'll be fine."

Unfortunately, it's not that simple.

Hackers don't swipe credentials to access that same service; they take them knowing many passwords are recycled out of laziness or convenience. The average consumer uses a password four times, so cracking your forgotten Food Network account gains entry to three more platforms; is one of them your bank, your credit card, your firm's case management software, or file sharing service?

DETECTION

Early detection of compromised credentials is critical but often proves elusive. With breaches regularly undetected or ignored, victims remain unaware that their passwords have been stolen and thus take no countermeasures.

Thieves then bundle your credentials and sell them on the dark web to hackers whose algorithms try accounts all over the Internet, looking to get a hit and steal your data, your money, or your identity.

So, how can you tell if your credentials have been compromised?

Relying on service providers to quickly detect breaches or promptly provide notification has proven a losing strategy — the only way to get ahead of the problem is to monitor the dark web itself.

SCANNING THE SHADOWS

Monitoring the dark web is like keeping tabs on the underworld to see what ill-gotten goods are available: if your credentials are there, it's clear they've been stolen, and time for protective action. This monitoring must be done continuously so you can know as soon as your data shows up in places you don't want it to be.

Credential antics are not victimless crimes but often leave clueless victims — don't be one of them. Discovering that your credentials are compromised before the damage is done can be the difference between life and death for yourself and your firm.

TIP #26:

DARK WEB MONITORING: A BRIGHT IDEA FOR KEEPING YOUR DATA PROTECTED

Credential corruption is the most invasive menace among today's many cybersecurity threats. When criminals have your passwords, they can infiltrate your systems and empty accounts before you know you're in danger. Even with security measures such as phishing prevention, password vaults, and remote malware scans, the threat remains from previous breaches or hacks to your third-party services.

Thoroughly ensuring your info isn't exposed requires spying on the bad guys who sell it by utilizing proactive dark web monitoring.

Every week seems to bring news of another corporate data breach. Target, LinkedIn, Morgan Stanley, Equifax, and T-Mobile have all recently surrendered sensitive records concerning hundreds of millions of clients.

After such breaches, stolen data is sold to criminal coders armed with algorithms designed to open every online account they can find. Hackers don't attack LinkedIn hoping to mess with your resume. They repurpose vital information to access your bank, network, or email — scary stuff.

Scarier still is being unaware that your identity is for sale.

This shady economy lives on the "dark web," an underground marketplace for nefarious transactions inaccessible to the average Internet user. But with the right tools and know-how, dark web monitoring can patrol that muck, so you don't have to.

Best-in-class monitoring services include continuously scanning the creepiest corners of the digital underworld and detecting in real-time whether your data has been offered to professional hackers.

Your firm will be notified immediately of any compromised credentials, providing crucial time to take countermeasures and secure your accounts before others access them.

You can't prevent hacks against outside parties, but monitoring the dark web for your data provides notice when these breaches affect your credentials, limiting your firm's exposure.

You should also probably double-check your LinkedIn resume, just in case.

HOW TO SECURE YOUR LAW FIRM FROM THE DARK WEB

I know the idea of a shadowy, clandestine alternative internet sounds like the plot of a '90s sci-fi movie, but that's what the modern-day dark web is today.

It's not a matter of *if* your firm is breached; it's a matter of *when*.

How far are cybercriminals willing to go to get your data? How many hoops do they have to jump through along the way?

A cybercriminal, who wears a nice suit, not a black hoodie, would probably answer with: "As many as I need to because your data is worth that much on the dark web. Click this link to see how much..."

Stop! Don't click that link!

Why is the dark web the home of hacking mischief?

Unless you know how to protect your identity, the dark web isn't safe for amateurs to roam.

It's not a perfect analogy, but the dark web resembles the stray iceberg that sunk the Titanic. The captain had no way of knowing that most of the danger lay underneath the waves; it looked safe.

The takeaway for law firms and their law practices is that the dark web remains a concern despite the good guys' best efforts. Researchers estimate the deep web is 400 to 500 times larger than the internet that most of us know; the dark web thrives as a subset of the deep web.

But the deep web isn't inherently bad.

What is terrible — and potentially financially devastating for law practices who suffer a data breach — are the shady characters exploiting it as a medium to sell stolen data and who knows what else.

Complicating matters further, the scripts being used have also changed, according to a recent Malwarebyte's report. For instance, security researchers discovered that the new malware could scrape payment processing data without compromising endpoints.

ANYONE CAN GET HACKED.

When businesses suffer a breach, it's usually from a more massive breach you had no control over. Don't get me wrong. Using cloud services is standard practice, but you must pick up the pieces on your own when they get hacked.

WHAT'S THE WORST THAT COULD HAPPEN IF OR WHEN YOUR FIRM GETS HACKED?

Simply put, the worst is that you might be on the hook to pay enormous penalties for compromising your clients' data. But the damage can be more than financial; an alarming data breach can ruin your firm's reputation that you worked so hard to build.

Stolen credentials on the dark web aren't solely a problem for big firms because small and medium-sized practices get hit, too. In fact, hackers *prefer* to go after small and medium-sized firms since they often don't have as many protections in place, if any.

OK, NOW WHAT CAN I DO TO PROTECT MYSELF ON THE DARK WEB?

Check to see if your credentials have already been compromised with a dark web report. If anything turns up (which happens nine times out of 10), complete the following steps:

- Reset Your Passwords.
- Reset Any Company Wide Log-ins/Passwords.
- Turn on MFA (Multi-Factor Authorization).

- Promote Awareness — communicate the information, so others are aware.
- Implement Cybersecurity and Phishing Email Training.
- Consistent dark web monitoring and reporting.

BUT HOW WILL I BE SAFE IN THE FUTURE?

Having continuous 24/7 monitoring of your credentials on the dark web is imperative. You will receive a notification as soon as your information turns up in a shadowy, illegal forum. You can use the tips above to stay one step ahead of the cybercriminals.

TIP #28:
REMOTE CONTROL

With the rise of remote working, cybersecurity risks have risen exponentially as employers attempt to create cyber-safe working environments that can be implemented by teams that may be fully or partially remotely working. The following few tips will highlight some risks of remote work.

And I don't mean the danger of an impromptu Zoom meeting.

RISE/RISKS OF REMOTE WORKING

You may have trusted your firm's cybersecurity, but as cybersecurity threats continue to grow year over year, it's time to address how this is exacerbated by remote working. Recent reports share that half of all organizations experienced security incidents tied to expanded out-of-office log-ins. With remote work options continuing to grow, how can you accommodate it safely?

REMOTE REASSURANCE

You can implement several quick fixes to increase security with minimal effort; most we've addressed before, but they're significant in the context of working remotely.

1. Always connect remotely using a Virtual Private Network (aka VPN).
2. Protect your credentials with unique passwords and multi-factor authentication.
3. Only share sensitive data via secure transfer services rather than email attachments.

In the longer run, it's critical to reassess your law firm's security relative to the altered working landscape, and proactively monitor against emerging threats at the office and remotely.

TIP #29:
IT'S TIME FOR YOUR SHOT

Just as vaccines bring COVID under control, the world is on the cusp of another pandemic: Ransomware.

That's not hyperbole, but congressional testimony from the Cybersecurity and Infrastructure Security director. His assessment is backed by the numbers showing that ransomware attacks are only increasing in recent years and shutting down many different organizations, including schools, corporations, and even a major east coast pipeline.

Ransomware is a catchy name for tools that enable digital blackmail; hackers steal data and lock out access, then demand payment to restore systems and secrets.

Experts attribute the rise in attacks to increased remote working and phishing opportunities driven by quarantine conditions.

Dark web entities have exploited these vulnerabilities, and their actions are only expected to grow more sophisticated, frequent, and aggressive.

Law firm security has become a particularly lucrative target as attorneys hold sensitive data. So, what can you do to protect yourself?

Many steps will sound familiar but are more crucial than ever in light of growing risks:

- Keep all software patched and updated
- Use unique passwords and secure connections
- Back up all data offsite
- Regularly scan for infections

And if that sounds like a lot to do yourself, find a professional provider to ensure these security precautions are implemented. There are enough worrying headlines in the world; don't let your firm be the next one to succumb to cyber threats.

TIP #30:
EVEN MICROSOFT
CAN'T LOCK THE GATES

The determination that a recent Microsoft Exchange hack was the work of bad actors has put that massive breach back in the headlines, worrying businesses of all sizes.

The encouraging news is that small and midsized firms using cloud-based email servers likely escaped catastrophe this time. More frightening is how pervasive cybercrime remains when even a tech giant like Microsoft can fall prey.

It's a stark reminder that every business — regardless of size — must remain on guard against cybersecurity threats or enlist the aid of vigilant professionals.

According to authorities, the hackers exploited unpatched systems and stolen credentials to pull off the bold Exchange hack. The breach affected over 100,000 email accounts (including small businesses, local governments, healthcare companies, and manufacturers), resulting in espionage and ransom demands.

What can you do besides nervously monitor the news?

As a law firm reliant on outside tech platforms, you can't secure external infrastructures, but there are steps you can take to protect your interests.

- By promptly identifying, verifying, and installing critical security updates/patches on every device in your organization, you can avoid software exploits that hackers rely on to get into your system.
- By ensuring your team uses unique, complex passwords backed by multi-factor authentication (most efficiently implemented with a password manager), you can shut down the damage caused by compromised credentials.
- You needn't be at the mercy of ransomware when you regularly back up business-critical email data on separate secure sites.
- Maintaining a cybersecurity insurance policy allows you to retain experienced assistance and financial protection should the worst scenario unfold.

These steps will help you to protect yourself, your reputation, your clients and your business, making future news headlines less scary.

PROACTIVE POLICIES & PLANNING

ALWAYS BE PREPARED
(WITH A CYBERSECURITY PLAN)

"A byte of prevention is worth a gig of cure," is what Ben Franklin might say if he were still alive and publishing today (think Bezos, with slightly more hair).

OK, the imagery is odd, but the adage remains sound — and is especially relevant when it comes to getting hacked.

Whether facing cybersecurity threats, equipment failure, or improbable scenarios (like a pandemic), the most critical steps for protecting your business are those taken well ahead of a crisis.

You can save significant headaches later by investing minimum time now — let me show you how.

Every firm (regardless of size — yes, solos, small firms and mid-sized, too) need an IT security plan that establishes expectations, anticipates challenging scenarios, and lays out best-practice responses.

That's not just a recommendation but a requirement for regulatory compliance in specific practice fields. Yet, according to a recent ABA report, only about 40% of small firms have such a plan in place.

If you're part of the plan-less 60%, don't delay any longer — enlist a consultant who understands your system, and it won't be a scary or complicated process.

The National Institute of Standards in Technology suggests that all IT plans feature a four-part framework:

1. **Preparation:** Anticipating issues, prescribing crisis protocol.
2. **Detection:** Defining critical factors for catching problems early.
3. **Containment:** Enacting protocol measures to counter the issue quickly.
4. **Assessment:** Post-incident evaluation of damage, initiation of remedies, and diagnosis of possible improvements.

While these general steps remain constant, their elements change according to equipment, software, firm size, and practice.

An easy way to do this is to find a customizable Cybersecurity Plan template that can be quickly tailored to any situation. IT contingency plans are necessary for the same reason as fire drills, so everyone understands their roles and requirements before stress clouds judgment and seconds are in short supply.

Having procedures in place provides peace of mind now, prevents panic later, and could save data, clients, and careers.

Like a spare tire, you'll hopefully never need it, but without it, you're attempting to drive a three-wheeled car.

That's why the Boy Scouts tell us to "Always Be Prepared," so take their advice, make a security plan, and maybe earn that technology merit badge.

STOLEN CREDENTIALS: WHAT NOW?

We've seen that Dark Web monitoring is the most effective method for swiftly detecting stolen credentials, but what should you do after discovering that you have compromised passwords?

First, follow advice from *The Hitchhiker's Guide to the Galaxy* and "Don't panic!" (carrying a towel is optional).

Next, you need to notify every affected account holder.

Don't get angry with the staff (or yourself); employees should be open about security lapses, and most thefts aren't even the victims' fault. Simply commit to quickly resetting all passwords related to the corrupted credentials.

Note: You'll want to change passwords that are an exact match, but should also reset variations of that password. For example, if nameofmypet was found. I would also change passwords like nam30fmypet or nameofmypet1!. These variations are easy for hackers to test and very predictable.

Changing passwords can be a tedious task, but don't delay. The first time I ran a dark web report on myself and saw the shocking amount of exposure, I spent hours resetting dozens of passwords, but it was a one-time inconvenience that has made it easier for me to sleep ever since.

While changing your passwords, remember **to create a unique password for every account** and use long strings to increase their strength. One simple method is to combine three unrelated words into a single password, like Pastrami-Gelato-Tortilla (sorry, I'm writing this at lunchtime).

Bonus: Once you have unique passwords for every account, your risk is siloed, and you'll never need to change more than one in response to future threats.

Instead of personally choosing and tracking countless passwords in a stack of sticky notes, I strongly suggest using a password manager (such as 1Password or LastPass). These services automatically generate and save unique passwords, autofill logins for quick access, and enable encrypted sharing of team credentials.

With hackers now locked out, you can assess whether they caused any damage.

Check all related accounts for altered data, withdrawn funds, or forged emails, and notify relevant institutions, authorities, or clients if anything is awry. A law firm cybersecurity plan will guide you through this protocol, and a cybersecurity insurance policy will protect against financial expenses incurred.

Facing vulnerability is a scary experience, but you get through it and are ready to guard against future breaches. Now change those passwords and reward yourself with a tasty PastramiGelatoTortilla.

TIP #33:
IN CASE OF EMERGENCY

It might not be exciting or flashy, but having a comprehensive cybersecurity plan is essential for any law firm. Cybersecurity is a growing concern for businesses of all sizes, and those in the legal profession are no exception. In today's digital world, law firms must protect their confidential client information, financial data and internal systems from cyber threats. A comprehensive cybersecurity plan can provide the necessary safeguards to keep a law firm's information secure.

Sometimes saving the day doesn't require a superhero, just a Boy Scout who showed up prepared. Business emergencies come in various forms, but every kind can threaten security. Natural disasters, ransomware threats, data hacks, facility damage, disgruntled employees, or global pandemics that force drastic work changes all put your data at risk. Once trouble arrives, there's no time to waste. It's the same reason we hold fire drills: to know what to do in a crisis. Whatever their size, law firms need emergency protocols spelling out best practices that limit damage during stressful scenarios. That's more than a recommendation in several practice fields; it's a regulatory requirement. Yet without time or expertise to draft such plans, only 40% of small firms have security policies in place.

It may seem overwhelming to draft up a cybersecurity plan, but there is no need to do it all yourself. Find a professional to help you implement it by supplying a cybersecurity protocol template and adapting it to your firm's specifics.

Spare tires aren't exciting either, but you don't want to be caught without one.

TIP #34:

BEWARE THE DREADED 'WARES

Previous tips have helped you secure your online accounts from catastrophic credential breaches, but what happens when the security battle suddenly makes its way to the home front?

Malware, ransomware, adware, and a vast array of viruses constantly seek to infiltrate your system — a virtual pack of "Ware-wolves" forever huffing and puffing at your front door.

The good news is that you can keep them at bay without the software getting in your way. Proactive scanning works quietly in the background to safely update your systems with security and software updates, performs regular maintenance, and scans for signs of trouble. Saving time and saving your butt.

Malicious infections most commonly gain access via exploitable holes in software — these holes are the reason for frequent prompting of patches, but the fixes themselves are often fraught with problems:

- Urgent updates rushed out without debugging may neutralize the immediate threat but create a host of secondary issues (think side effects for medicine).
- Patches designed for one program occasionally make them incompatible with another in your suite (conflicting prescriptions).
- Relying on employees to independently update devices can lead to lag time, leaving computers exposed to infection (forgetting to take your pills).

Luckily, there is a way to painlessly and easily keep your data safe from these viruses.

Find a proactive monitoring solution and check to make sure it does the following:

- Before releasing any patches or software updates, ensure that the solution provider checks them for flaws and compatibility issues.
- Confirm that they have been tested and verified before being remotely installed on any device.
- Ask if they have a solution to remove/remediate any uninvited "guests" found during the scanning process to protect against dangers that updating can't prevent.

Protecting online accounts is imperative, but don't relent when defending your home turf from adware, ransomware, and malware. And don't construct your walls from simple straw or sticks – fight the Big Bad Ware-wolves with the solid brick assurance of proactive scanning.

TIP #35:

LET'S GET 'CYBER' SMART WITH CYBERSECURITY AWARENESS TRAINING

Despite pop culture depictions, most data breaches don't involve brute-force computer hacks. Instead, cybercriminals rely on user carelessness, gullibility, or lack of threat awareness.

Humans are the weakest link in any security plan; impressive locks don't mean a thing if an employee unknowingly turns over the keys. That's why consistent training for you and your staff should be one of the first layers of a cybersecurity defense plan — a cracked foundation causes all else to tumble.

With a third of data breaches attributed to phishing and up to 90% tracing back to human error, training is as critical to cybersecurity as any firewall or countermeasure.

The problem is that most employees will skip or ignore boring cybersecurity lessons. Instead of lame lectures or death by PowerPoint, find a cybersecurity awareness training solution that uses animated storytelling techniques with clever characters and gamified elements that make information more memorable. The videos should be short, spaced about a month apart, and fun so employees will actually complete and remember the training.

Lessons should cover phishing detection, password protection, avoiding malware/ransomware, and best practices for email use, mobile security, browser fidelity, WiFi integrity, and more. This knowledge is power that helps your team thwart cybersecurity attacks before they ever access your system. It's critical to keep ahead of evolving hacker trends and be aware of the latest threats.

TIP #36:

BACK IT UP: DAILY DATA BACK-UPS

Found this in a fortune cookie: "Lawyer who represents themself has a fool for a client — and so does a lawyer who is fool enough not to backup data on a daily incremental basis."

I have no idea how the fortune cookie company managed to squeeze all that onto a tiny strip of paper — especially that last bit about daily data backup.

OK, just joking about the fortune cookie, but truthfully it is foolhardy to slack off on backing up data pertaining to your clients, cases, and business operations.

Daily incremental backup is essential, considering how ridiculously easy it is to lose data to theft, malicious attack, human error, system malfunctions, or natural disasters.

Consequently, the longer you let data backup slide, the greater your potential for peril.

What kind of peril? Oh, I dunno. Like the derailment of cases that were chugging merrily along toward victory until everything related to them suddenly vanished off your computers. Or like your formerly happy clients demanding your head on a spike (or at least enough compensation for lawyer malpractice to make your firm go belly up).

As I've warned, the data in your possession is sensitive and, therefore, must be aggressively protected. That's a fiduciary duty you owe your clients. No escaping that.

Daily incremental backing up is the simplest way to protect all the confidential information you are charged with safeguarding.

Who am I kidding? I know that daily data backup can be a pain because it is, after all, a chore, but it is seriously worth it in the end.

TIP #37:

LAST LINE OF DEFENSE

"Everybody has a plan until they get punched in the mouth."
~ Michael Gerard Tyson

Iron Mike is rarely credited as a deep thinker and is certainly no IT expert, but his message should hit hard with anyone who believes they've accounted for every dire contingency. Spoiler alert: you haven't.

We've already examined several ways to optimize your protection online and off: safeguarding accounts, updating software, browsing smarter, using private networks, and encrypting data, but sometimes you slip up, or chaos finds a way to win.

So, what happens when all else fails?

Fear not. There's one more step that will cover your ass and soothe your psyche in case the worst-case scenario plays out — data backups.

 Most of us have suffered a data loss at some point, so we know how much of a nightmare it is!

Whether victimized by hackers, thieves, human error, or hardware/software meltdown, it's a sickening feeling to realize you've lost client files, precious memories, or the brief you spent all night writing.

However, if your data is reliably backed up, such catastrophes become mere inconvenience... and that process has never been more straightforward.

Some choose to backup files locally using external hard drives and programs like Time Machine, but this is not recommended as a sole solution: hard drives have limited space, sporadic connectivity, and are just as susceptible to theft/fire/failure as your laptop.

If you want to keep an extra copy of critical files on an encrypted drive nearby, fine — but always have another backup off-site.

Your best bet is one of the numerous affordable cloud-based services available to back up your files automatically; they run in the background whenever you're online, uploading to limitless servers and cataloging several recent versions of your data in case of accidental deletion/overwriting.

You don't need to back up *everything* on your computer — operating systems, system files, and software can all be replaced — prioritize your client/firm files, your email/calendars/contacts, and other files that are uniquely yours (photos, music, etc.).

Think of it as an insurance policy — maybe you can't stop someone from hitting your car, lightning from striking your house, or your appendix from bursting. Still, a simple plan and minimal expenditure make life easier afterward. Backing up files does the same for whatever disaster may befall your data.

The response if/when it happens should be stoic:

"Well, that's annoying, but I know I have a backup and haven't lost anything."

Vs.

"OMG, what do I do?!!!"

It's always good to have peace of mind if you happen to get punched in the mouth.

FINAL THOUGHTS:
TAKING THE NEXT STEP TO PROTECT YOUR LAW FIRM

Congratulations on completing the book! You now have at your disposal 37 valuable tips to help you secure your firm from cyber criminals. As cyber threats continue to evolve and become more sophisticated, it is imperative that you stay one step ahead of them.

As an added bonus for those of you that made it this far, we have a Master Class cybersecurity webinar that you can use for yourself or to share valuable information with you team. Just go to **www.bobaguard.com/SSSTWebinar** to download the class.

While the tips you have learned so far are certainly effective in reducing your risk, it may feel overwhelming and/or not cost effective for you to implement these and everything else on your own to obtain a fully comprehensive cybersecurity plan. If you want to truly fortify your law firm's cybersecurity defenses, we highly recommend booking a strategy call with Bobaguard to learn more about our full suite of cybersecurity solutions and how we can provide the white glove service to implement and maintain these solutions for your firm.

Our cybersecurity solutions advisors can work with you to identify your law firm's specific needs and customize a cybersecurity plan that fits. With our state-of-the-art technology and advanced tools, you can rest assured that your law firm is protected from even the most advanced cyber threats.

ABOUT THE AUTHOR

Tom Lambotte is a cybersecurity expert who has been in the tech support industry for over a decade. He founded BobaGuard in 2019, which offers a suite of turnkey solutions to protect mid-size law firms from getting hacked.

Tom is also the CEO and Founder of GlobalMac IT, an established managed service provider specializing in serving lawyers nationwide who use Macs by implementing their Proven Process™. Tom's mission is to help entrepreneurs grow by leveraging technology. He has taken it upon himself to be a hero to small and mid-size law firms, at the intersection of technology adoption, efficiency, and security. BobaGuard was born out of a passion for making the latest cybersecurity solutions accessible and affordable to all lawyers, not just BigLaw.

Tom is the author of the ABA's "Macs in Law" and has been widely published by legal industry print and online publications. He also authored *Hassle-Free Mac IT Support for Law Firms* and *Legal Boost: Big Profits Through an IT Transformation*. Tom's weekly blog, Stupid Simple Security Tips, provides actionable and simplified strategies to protect firms from getting hacked.

His third company, OneDay Workweek, is a boutique consultancy that works closely with CEO & COOs to develop and implement the structure needed to create a self-managing company. Lastly, Tom created a collaboration with Mike Koenigs, Ai Mastery Series, to help CEOs and their teams implement and leverage AI into their companies.

He lights up a room with his contagious charm and love for all things family. He may be the proud dad of four sweet adopted kids (and two cute French Bulldog puppies) and husband to his fantastic wife, but he lives an adventurous lifestyle as well! Every day brings new adventures in Chardon, Ohio, where you can find this active family man at home, foraging for mushrooms, or out exploring hiking trails near the Lake Erie coastline or sampling the best ice cream shops in Chagrin Falls with his family.

www.bobaguard.com
www.globalmacit.com
www.myonedayworkweek.com

Made in the USA
Middletown, DE
23 April 2023

29042559R00086